Mount Grace F......

Glyn Coppack and Mark Douglas

CONTENTS

Tour of the Priory

OVERVIEW AND SETTING

Mount Grace lay on the medieval road from York to Durham. The modern entry track has its origins in the medieval track that led off this road to the priory gatehouse. The entrance to the charterhouse (Carthusian monastery) today is through the later house, built in the shell of the early 15th-century guest house. Although extended and heavily remodelled at the end of the 19th century, many features of the 17th-century house and its medieval predecessor remain.

The medieval guest house enclosed the west side of the priory's semi-public Inner Court. To the north of the Inner Court were the kitchen, refectory and prior's house, and to the east the priory church. To the north of the church is the Great Cloister, with its cells for the monks (choir monks). South and east of the church is the Lesser Cloister, which housed the lay brothers (*conversi*). The service buildings of the Inner Court are on its south side. The original sense of enclosure in the monastery is now lost: the open area between the guest house and the church originally comprised walled and gated yards. These became gardens and service yards (the remains of which are seen today) of the later house.

Remarkably, some medieval buildings survive to roof height. Those that are visible only as foundations were taken down in the late 16th and 17th centuries, the stone to be sold or used elsewhere. The cloister enclosure survives because it became a walled garden, and the Inner Court a farmyard. Remarkably the church was not intentionally destroyed but left to fall into ruin.

Above: A Carthusian monk praying in a landscape, in an Italian manuscript of the early 15th century. The Carthusian order had spread from Continental Europe to Britain two and a half centuries earlier

Below: Mount Grace Priory from the south-west. The Inner Court is towards the bottom of the picture, with the church and Great Cloister beyond

Facing page: Looking north across the low ruins of the east cloister wall towards the reconstructed monk's cell

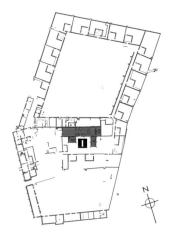

MONASTIC RUINS

The priory was essentially a series of enclosures controlling access to the monks in their cells to ensure their seclusion. The Inner Court was the interface with the outside world and the priory's estate. The church, also enclosed, lay at the centre of the precinct with, roughly, the Inner Court and lay brothers' cells on one side, and the monks' cells on the other.

◼ THE CHURCH AS FIRST BUILT

Unlike monks of other orders, Carthusians said most of their offices in their cells. Their churches are consequently small and plain compared with those of other orders. The first church at Mount Grace was a rectangular building of four bays, 26.8m long and 7.6m wide inside. It formed in effect two churches, that of the monks in the eastern two bays (later the choir) and the lay brothers in the western bays (later the nave). These were separated by a cross passage screened on both sides with a loft above: a combined rood and pulpitum screen typical of Carthusian churches throughout Europe.

The lay brothers and guests entered by the west door from the yard in front of the church, the monks through a cross passage from the Great Cloister to the north. Their door can still be seen, although it has been moved slightly west. A door in the south wall was blocked when the church was remodelled. All but the east wall of this first church survive almost to full height, and two of its windows survive in part. One, in the west bay of the south wall, retains its western jamb and part of the cill and springing of its head. Excavation recovered some of its tracery. The other, between the third and fourth bays of the north wall, is blocked, but its cill is set low down, indicating that the monks' stalls did not have canopies.

Below right: The church today. The west door, to the bottom left, dates from the first building of the church c.1400

Below: *Reconstruction drawings of the church from the south-west*
A *c.1400; as first built*
B *c.1425; bell tower has been built*

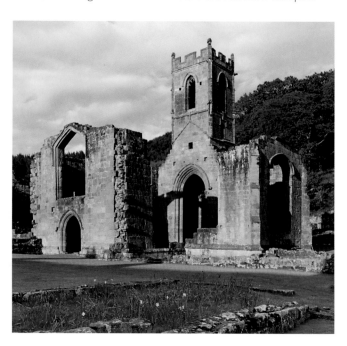

▮ THE CHURCH ENLARGED

The second period of building followed the refounding and enlargement of the priory by Thomas Beaufort (c.1377–1426) in 1415. Beaufort – grandson of a king, uncle to the future king, and half-brother to the one after that – had the church extended to make it a fit burial place for himself.

The screens of the cross passage were rebuilt in stone and carried up to support a small bell tower reached by a stair turret against the south wall. To accommodate this the south door of the passage was blocked and the north door moved. On the west side (the nave side) a timber rood loft was built and below it two altars were built, one on each side of the tower arch.

This new tower survives intact, apart from its floors and roof, and has three stages. The lower stage was a room with openings overlooking the nave to the west and monks' choir to the east. The middle stage had windows to north and south and a door into the roof space over the choir. The upper stage was the belfry. It had transomed windows on each face below an embattled parapet with corner pinnacles and waterspouts.

As well as this new bell tower the monks' choir was extended by a bay to the east. The original window in the north wall was blocked. Two pairs of three-light windows were inserted much higher in the old north wall, their cills above the canopies of the monks' new choir stalls and above the roof gutter of the chapter house abutting outside. The south wall (now gone), probably similarly had its old windows blocked and new windows inserted, but set lower, above the line of the vestry roof.

Above: The church from the south. The delicate three-light windows can be seen in the remains of the monks' choir

Below: Reconstruction drawings of the church from the south-west

C c.1475; burial chapels added

D c.1500; vestry to the south-east replaced by a third burial chapel

Above: The second bay of the choir in the north wall. The blocked area of the original window can be seen below the later three-light window, which was set higher up to avoid the canopies of the new choir stalls

The new work is now reduced to low walling, but parts of the window that was in the east wall have been excavated and suggest that it was full length. At the junction of the old and new work doors were inserted, in the north wall leading into the chapter house and in the south into a vestry (later a burial chapel) that projected from the south wall.

The layout of the choir can be seen in the features remaining in the floor and walls. To north and south are the bases of the choir stalls, and shallow grooves in the north wall show the position of their high canopies. Between the choir stalls, and extending up to the sanctuary step, was a tiled floor, in the centre of which is Thomas Beaufort's tomb. He was buried here in 1427.

2 Burial Chapels

The strict piety of the Carthusians attracted the patronage of many: initially in return for the saying of memorial Masses, and later for burial places in their small churches, which had to be extended for the purpose. In the late 15th century burial chapels were added to the nave at Mount Grace, first on the south

Prayers for the Dead

Accepting burials brought the priory community income and respectability, while it gave their patrons the hope of eternal salvation.

The Carthusians' reputation for piety and for the power of their prayers is reflected in many northern English wills from the mid 15th century on: money or other gifts were left to the monks in exchange for prayers and memorial Masses.

Initially, requests for burial came only from members of the Ingleby family, the joint founder of the priory, but by the later 15th century requests were more widespread and accompanied by substantial gifts. In 1500, for instance, Thomas Darell of Sessay gave his house and land at East Harlsey for his burial and 10 marks (£6.66) for two priests to celebrate the anniversary of his death for seven years.

Below: A reminder that death reduces all to the same state – even those able to afford splendid tombs such as this; a detail from a manuscript produced at Mount Grace between 1460 and 1500

side and then on the north, with large arches cut into the nave walls that required the removal of a window on the south side. Both chapels were divided from the nave by wooden screens and had altars with substantial altarpieces; their fixings survive in the blind east walls. Graves are clearly visible in their floors.

In the early 16th century a third chapel was added. This was built on the south side of the monks' choir on the site of the vestry, retaining the vestry door. A new vestry was built to the west, south of the cross passage. This chapel contained two altars with a table tomb between them and was probably built for the Strangways family of East Harlsey, two of whom are known to have been buried at Mount Grace in 1532. Similar burial chapels at the London Charterhouse are described as having interiors panelled with wainscot and elaborate altarpieces bearing statues of the saints to which they were consecrated, an elaboration not required by the Carthusians but by their patrons.

The new vestry was entered by a new door from the southern burial chapel in the nave, and though largely demolished, its extent can be seen from the pecking of the masonry where its inside walls were plastered.

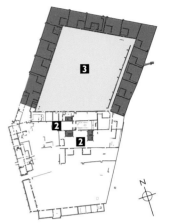

▣ GREAT CLOISTER

North of the church, occupying its own terrace, is the Great Cloister. Around this space the individual cells for the monks and the principal communal buildings of the charterhouse were built. The extent of the terrace, laid out at the foundation of the priory, indicates the substantial scale on which the monks intended to build, though it was to take almost the whole life of the priory to achieve it.

Above: A fragment inscribed with the method of obtaining a pardon from purgatory, found at Mount Grace
Below: The Great Cloister

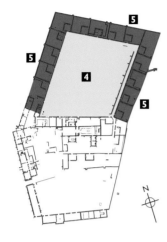

Above: The arms of Archbishop Richard Scrope on the entrance to Cell 2. Scrope may have funded the building of this cell

Below: South wall of the Great Cloister

A Entrance to the chapter house and church

B Entrance to Cell 23

C Food hatch to Cell 23

D Laver

E Food hatch to Cell 22

F Entrance to Cell 22

G Entrance to prior's cell

H Food hatch to prior's cell

I Base of oriel window

4 Cloister Garden

The cloister garth (central space) of a charterhouse comprised a garden and the monks' cemetery, which at Mount Grace was probably in the south-east corner in front of the cell of the sacrist ('housekeeper' of both the church and chapter house). Priors seem to have been buried in the south cloister alley, the earliest outside the door of the first prior's cell.

The garth was surrounded by covered alleys, the roofs supported on corbels that remain in the enclosing walls. The alleys served simply to link the cells with the church, chapter house and refectory, not as the centre of communal life as in other orders. They were originally built in timber. In the 1420s parts of the north, west and south alleys were rebuilt in stone. Finally in the late 15th century the east alley was rebuilt to a slightly different design. Parts, however, remained in timber and some windows were glazed (possibly gifts from patrons) and others were not. At the centre of the cloister was an elegant octagonal water tower (nothing of which is now visible) built in the 1420s by the masons who built the first stone arcade wall.

5 Monks' Cells

Although the development of the cells was piecemeal, their total number – 15 – was intended from the start. The first cells were of timber: two, for the prior and the sacrist, at either end of the south alley, and seven more on the east side and part of the north side of the cloister by 1412. Rebuilding in stone began in about 1420 with Cell 1 at the south-east corner,

extending to Cell 7 as money became available, followed by Cells 15 to 9 on the west, and finally Cell 8 in about 1480.

Each cell had two storeys, stood in the corner of its own garden, and was entered through a door in the otherwise blind wall facing the cloister. Beyond the entry passage the cell was subdivided by timber partitions to form three rooms: a living room with a fireplace and a four-light window (Cell 8 has an additional single-light window, allowable because of an original mistake in its layout); a bedroom and oratory (private chapel) with a single-light window; and a study with a four-light window. All the windows looked onto the garden at the back of the cell.

Within the entry passage, but accessed from the living room, was a stair leading to the upper floor, which was a general purpose workroom. A door opposite the stair opened onto a part-open passage running the length of the cell garden to a latrine in the outer wall. A door at the other end of the entry passage led to a short private cloister alley along the cloister wall, looking onto the monk's garden.

In the 16th century two additional cells, 22 and 23, were built between the church and the south cloister alley above cellars that raised them to the level of the Great Cloister. Their layout was the same as the other cells but compressed to fit difficult sites, and they had no gardens. The oratory of Cell 22 was built into the west wall of the north burial chapel.

Top left: *Looking west over the garden of Cell 6. A drain in the garden of the adjacent Cell 5 can be seen on the left*

Top right: *A Carthusian monk at devotions in the garden of his cell, as depicted in an English Carthusian manuscript produced at Mount Grace between 1460 and 1500*

Above: *The latrine of a monk's cell*

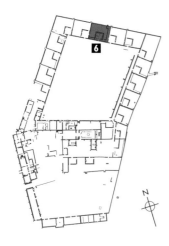

Above right: The bedroom of the reconstructed monk's cell, with its window overlooking the cell garden
Below: Satchel fastener found in the garden of Cell 8. Such a fastener would have secured the satchel held by the monk depicted on page 9
Bottom: Garden of the reconstructed monk's cell

Facing page: Reconstruction of Mount Grace Priory as it may have looked in about 1530, with Cell 8 cutaway in the foreground

6 Reconstructed Monk's Cell

Cell 8 was rebuilt by Sir Lowthian Bell between 1901 and 1905. It was refitted by English Heritage in the late 1980s, its garden and galleries based on archaeological evidence and plants available in the 16th century, and its furnishings on contemporary Carthusian illustrations or surviving examples.

It is entered, as were the other cells, by a door with an L-shaped hatch in its east jamb. Food and other necessities could be passed through the hatch from the cloister alley without any communication. Shields on the hood moulding of the door were probably painted with the arms of the patron who funded the cell. The Carthusians used letters, which would have been painted on the west door jamb, to identify their cells (starting at 'A' for the prior; the numbers in use today were given in the 1890s). West of the entrance is a door to a glazed private cloister with a suspended wooden floor; excavation confirmed that most cells had wooden floors. The door to the east leads onto a gallery to the garden and latrine.

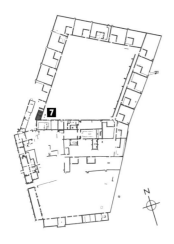

The living room, where the monk ate, has a large fireplace. It was the only heated room in the cell. Two doors opposite the fire lead to a study, with a large window, and a bedroom and oratory with a small window. The cell was a private monastery where the monk said his offices and celebrated Mass. For manual work he had the garden and a workroom on the upper floor, but many monks were copyists – their manual work was copying books. Finds from the garden indicate that one of the monks who lived in this cell was a bookbinder.

7 Priory Prison

In the south-west corner of the cloister is a much-altered building of the early 15th century. It has a single room on each floor and was entered by a now-blocked door in the corner of the cloister alley. This was the prison for monks who had

Life of a Carthusian Monk

The purpose of Carthusian life was total withdrawal from the world to serve God by personal devotion and privation. Carthusian monks followed the same daily round of seven offices as other orders, but uniquely they only celebrated the night office of Matins and afternoon office of Vespers together regularly, and Mass less frequently. Otherwise they said their offices and celebrated Mass alone in their cells.

Similarly, they ate in the refectory only on Sundays, feast days and the day of the burial of a brother. Normally, food and drink were brought to their cells by a lay brother and passed through the hatch beside the door. They regularly fasted, and often drank water, which was supplied to each cell by a tap.

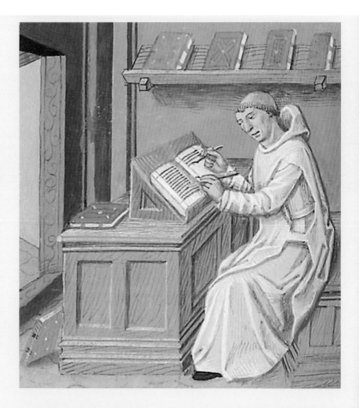

The cell provided for all their needs, particularly space to meditate, read, and work. Documents and the evidence of excavation show what 'trades' the monks followed. One, Sir Thomas Goldwynne, was a weaver and came from London with his loom and household goods in 1519; others, from the evidence of pens and oyster shells full of coloured pigments, copied and illuminated manuscripts. One was a bookbinder, with tools and book fittings.

The monks ate no meat except fish (which they considered vegetarian), though their guests were served other meat, which required two kitchens. High-quality imported pottery tableware has been found, and excavation of the disturbed the peace or tried to abscond. Usually, monks were sent to another house for correction. In 1439 John Welles of London was held at Mount Grace, as was for some years in the late 1450s William Everton of Hinton, whose weakness for women, despite his vows, had him passed from house to house in the hope of his reform. In 1528 London Charterhouse accepted William Barker, who had fled Mount Grace, in exchange for their monk Alnett Hales whose mental illness disturbed every community who took him in.

In the late 15th century the building ceased to be a prison. It was doubled in size and its door moved to access a new stair to the first floor, probably the priory library, itself connected to the upper floor of Cell 15 (that of the librarian, if the first floor was the library). A second door, possibly added later, led from the library to the refectory. The ground floor became a cellar.

Above: A monk apparently with a weakness for the woman beside him in the stocks sharing his punishment; detail from an English manuscript of the 14th century

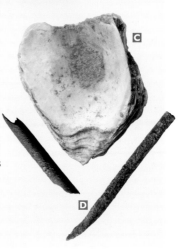

kitchen has shown that the main elements of the monks' diet were fish, pulses and eggs, though they could grow other vegetables in their gardens. Bread and beer were supplied by the lay brothers.

Above: The study and writing desk of the reconstructed monk's cell

Above left: A Carthusian monk writing; detail of a French manuscript c.1490

Right: Finds from Mount Grace Priory

A Corner of a book cover found in Cell 8, the bookbinder's cell

B One of a number of lead strips, reading in reverse 'Jesus Nazarenus', found in Cells 13 and 15. They were used by the monks to make plaster tokens for pilgrims

C Shell, with traces of pigment still visible, found in Cell 12

D Remains of two pens found in Cells 11 and 13

Priory Diet

Excavation of the monks' kitchen revealed evidence for the community's diet. Flesh and fowl were prohibited, but the monks ate fish, the skeletons of which were trampled into the floor. This unappealing custom of leaving the waste to rot on the floor preserved a record of the sea and estuarial fish eaten in the 15th century. It preserved, too, among the fishbones, a human toe, presumably cut off when a knife was dropped. Seal bones from the kitchen suggest that seals were considered fish. The guest house had its own, adjacent, kitchen that served meat. Its interior was destroyed in 1900.

Food was supplied to the monks' cells daily as well as to the refectory when it was used, and to the guest hall. While the monks had high-quality tableware, the kitchen had basic pottery and cooking vessels of iron and brass.

Below: Monks at refectory, in a mid 15th century Italian fresco. The cat and dog are squabbling over a fish tossed to the floor

Left and below: A spoon and German stoneware drinking pot, found at Mount Grace in Cell 8

Below: The food hatch and doorway to the prior's cell, with the projecting base of an oriel window that once lit the upper floor

8 Prior's Cell

West of the church was a range that contained, at its west end, the prior's cell and at its east, the refectory, which was built in about 1400. The prior's cell was simply a larger version of a monk's cell, with an entry passage along the cloister wall and three ground-floor rooms – living room, bedroom and oratory, and study – divided by timber partitions on stone cill-walls (low stone walls built to carry timber partitions). The prior had a hall on the floor above for entertaining important guests and patrons. His cell was adjacent to a passage through the range from the Inner Court to the Great Cloister, to which he would have held the key and granted access.

In the 1470s the prior's cell was relocated to the refectory in the eastern half of the range. It was partitioned into two ground-floor rooms and floored over to provide him with a hall and bedchamber on an upper storey, with an oriel window looking out onto the Great Cloister.

9 Refectory

The original refectory was a small, two-bay hall open to the roof with traceried windows in its south wall. Here the monks ate together only on Sundays, feast days and the day of the burial of a brother. It was entered on the west through a small door in a passage onto the cloister garth. Inside it was painted white and had a mortar floor. It was a plain, simple building, unlike the impressive refectories of other orders, which had large doors to the cloister and tiled floors.

In the 1470s the refectory was moved to the prior's old first-floor hall in the west of the range, closer to the kitchen. The passage through the range was converted to a stair to the new refectory and its southern door was blocked. The ground floor of the former prior's cell was altered to become a preparation area for the kitchen. It may have been the smell from the kitchen that had the prior move his cell to the east.

10 Chapter House

As the place where weekly business was conducted and discipline administered, the chapter house was central to monastic life. Its name comes from the routine of reading a chapter of the Rule of St Benedict before meetings, which were held on Sundays with all of the community attending.

The chapter house was built in the 1420s together with the extension of the church to which it is attached and from which it could be entered. It was also accessible from the Great Cloister through a little garden on the north side of the church with a covered gallery. Little remains of the chapter house, and no trace of its fittings, though there would have been an altar. Steps and a door in the east wall led up to the sacrist's cell, for he was responsible for the preparation (of the sacrament, candles and altar cloth, and so on) of both the church and chapter house.

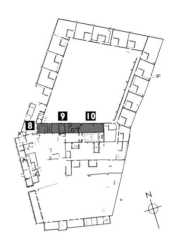

Below: A Carthusian reading; detail of a 16th-century Italian fresco. On Sundays the monks gathered in the chapter house, where a chapter of the Rule of St Benedict was read

Bottom: Remains of the chapter house. The steps on the right led into the cloister

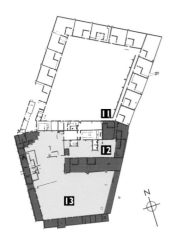

*Below: Remains of the substantial
fireplace of the sacrist, who was
ranked third in status at the priory*
*Bottom: Looking east across the
remains of the Lesser Cloister. Cell 17
is in the foreground*

11 Sacrist's Cell

The sacrist (third after the prior and procurator in seniority) was responsible for all care and management of the church, chapter house and the monks' cemetery in the cloister garden. His cell was always close to these parts of the monastery; at Mount Grace it was at the east end of the south range, the first of the monks' cells to be built in stone. Its cloister door cill had to be raised when the cloister alleys were laid out in the 1420s and in the 1470s, when the Lesser Cloister was built in stone, the north-east angle of the cell was cut back.

The only wall of the cell that remains to any height is the east, which has a fine fireplace and an offset that marks the first floor. Instead of a private cloister the sacrist had a stone-built corridor linked to the chapter house. Otherwise his cell was identical to the others of the Great Cloister. It remained the sacrist's cell until the closure of the priory.

12 LESSER CLOISTER

Outside the Great Cloister, to the east and south of the church, are the remains of six further cells built in the late 15th century, apparently replacing earlier timber ones. These were for the lay brothers, who ran the domestic life of the priory and acted as servants to the monks. Their cells are smaller than those of the monks, and had no upper storey, but were similarly divided by timber partitions into an entry passage, living room and bedroom. Each also had a walled garden, a private cloister and a latrine at the end of the garden gallery. A difference still visible today is the form of the fireplace: in these cells it projected into the living room; it is not known why.

Left: *Illustration of a lay brother taking food to the hatch of a choir monk*
Below: *An early 16th-century urinal found in Cell 8. No doubt a lay brother would have collected it from the hatch (urine was kept for tanning, typically to make parchment)*

Lives of the Lay Brothers

The lay brothers, or *conversi*, were essentially servants subject to monastic discipline. They did the manual work of the house, leaving the choir monks free to pray, meditate and study.

Originally housed in a separate but adjacent monastery, by the late 15th century they lived in the same house as the monks and obeyed the same rules. They were the cooks, bakers, brewers, gatekeepers and cleaners of the monastery, and its contact with the outside world and the estate. They were the responsibility of the most senior monk after the prior, the procurator, who also managed the priory's estates, guests and donates (those affiliated to the order).

Some of the lay brothers may have come from gentry families. In the 12th century some bishops retired to become Carthusian lay brothers, showing that it was an honourable rank, for supporting the choir monks was itself a way of serving God.

The building of the Lesser Cloister was a gradual process. The cloister wall and Cells 20 and 21 were the first to be built, probably replacing earlier temporary timber cells. Cells 17 to 19 were built next, butting against the cloister wall, almost certainly also replacing earlier timber cells. Finally, in the early 16th century, Cell 16 was built between the Lesser Cloister and the west end of the church. So limited was this cell's space that its garden and latrine lay on the other side of the cloister alley, alongside Cell 17. No trace survives of the cloister arcade. It was probably of timber. The Lesser Cloister had a door to the Inner Court at its west end, and a narrow passage into the Great Cloister.

Below: *The lay brothers were the cooks, bakers, brewers and cleaners of the priory; in this illustration of 1475 from Nuremberg a cook is shown at work over his pots and pans*

🄴 INNER COURT

The service ranges of the charterhouse occupied three sides of an enclosed yard, the Inner Court, that formed its own terrace to the south of the Lesser Cloister. The Inner Court was entered by a gatehouse and must originally have been defined by a wooden fence or bank and ditch before the tall precinct wall was built in the 1420s.

Above: The kiln house and granary

A Remains of the kiln

B Sockets for floor joists

C Granary

Below: The common stable in the
south range; one of the grooves cut to
support a manger is circled

14 East Range

The brewhouse and bakehouse of the priory formed the east range of the Inner Court. Sockets in the outer wall for its main floor joints show that it had two storeys and was six bays long, but it has not been excavated and its exact layout is unknown. In the south-east corner of the court was a stone-lined tank fed by a spring that provided water to this part of the priory.

15 South Range: Granary

At the east end of the south range was a granary, a standard monastic provision. It occupied three floors, with a grain-drying kiln in its east room. With the bakehouse and brewhouse it was capable of supplying all the bread and beer required daily by the house. This building was retained after the Suppression and some elements, such as a wall across the eastern building that would have blocked a window, are post-monastic.

16 South Range: Common Stable

At the centre of the south range, beside the granary, was the common stable, with three doors to the Inner Court and two internal partitions. Here the priory's horses and those of guests were kept. Both the prior and the procurator had to attend to external business and their status required they went on horseback. Drains were provided at the backs of the stalls and the slots for the mangers can still be seen in the south wall.

The upper floor was another granary or a hayloft, reached by a ladder from the Inner Court. The stable, with its upper floor, was built in the 1470s, the earliest building of the south range. It and the service buildings alongside it were built against the outside of the precinct wall through which doors were knocked to the Inner Court. Probably wooden buildings had stood against the inside of the wall and were taken down to create more space in the Inner Court for the lay brothers' cells.

The last building of the south range to be built, in the early 16th century, was that to the west. It also had three doors to the court and an upper storey. It may have provided extra stabling but has not been excavated and its use is not known.

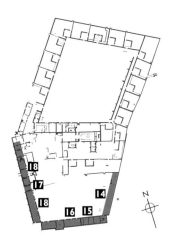

🔳 Gatehouse

The oldest building of the Inner Court, built in about 1400, is the gatehouse, which controlled access to this semi-public part of the priory. It stands at the centre of the west side of the court and comprised two vaulted bays, an outer porch and an inner gate hall. Two massive gates hung in the arch at the centre of the building where modern gates now hang.

Its upper storey was entered by a spiral stair in a turret on the north-east angle. The blocked door to the stair survives, but the upper storey was dismantled when the guest house to the north was modified in the early 17th century. Usually a monastery would have had a porter's lodge off the gate hall and the porter would have been a servant. But here there is no lodge: the porter would have been a lay brother who came from his cell to answer the bell at the gate.

🔳 Guest House

The house visible today was built within the shell of the 15th-century guest house. Its medieval layout was recovered during the restoration of the house from 1987 to 1988 (see page 40). As originally built in the 1420s it provided accommodation for guests, with four single rooms on the ground floor at the south end, each with a door and a square-headed window overlooking the Inner Court. Above these was better quality accommodation over two storeys: one or more suites of one or more rooms with a bedchamber on the upper floor. Every room was lit by two-light windows in both east and west walls. From the Inner Court an external timber stair led up to the south end of the first storey.

Above: The gatehouse, which was built in 1400, is the oldest building in the Inner Court
Below: The guest house south of the gatehouse, built in the 1470s. Above its five ground-floor rooms was a common dormitory for poorer guests

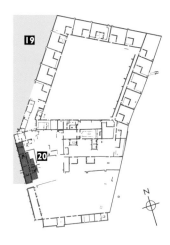

The guest hall was the central focus of the building. It was open to the roof and lit by single four-light windows in its east and west walls (now blocked, but clearly visible from outside). The north end of the building was the guest kitchen, with rooms above for the procurator. Another guest house was added in the 1470s to the south of the gatehouse. It had five ground-floor rooms facing the Inner Court below a common dormitory, reached by a stair from the Outer Court to the west, for poorer guests.

19 OUTER COURT

The farming and industrial activities (milling, smithing, general workmanship) of the priory took place in the Outer Court on the terrace west of the main priory buildings. The later gardens have obscured the southern half of this court, apart from the ruins of the water mill and its tail race near the north end of the guest house. Originally there were various farm buildings recorded as 'le grange' at the Suppression, a third guest house called 'le Inne', an ox house where the oxen used for ploughing were kept, and a series of late medieval fishponds, one of which has been re-watered. The fishponds incorporate the earthwork remains of a moated manor, probably the manor of Bordelbi granted to the Carthusians in 1398 (see page 25).

20 THE HOUSE

The house visible today was created in the early 17th century from the remains of the priory guest house. At the end of the 19th century the industrialist Sir Lowthian Bell refurbished and extended the house, guided by his interest in the Arts and Crafts movement. The house today remains much as he left it.

Below: Detail of the west entrance to the converted guest house, with the date 1654 and, to left and right, the letters T and L, for Thomas Lascelles, owner in the 17th century

Seventeenth-Century House

The 15th-century priory guest house faced eastwards onto the Inner Court, away from the outside world, as befitting a monastic building. When it was converted into a private residence in the 17th century the views to and from the outer approach, to the west, were emphasized instead, as typical of a domestic house.

The extent of the 17th-century house is seen in the main west front of today, with its added central porch and three bays of mullioned windows to either side. When converted, the roof was reconstructed, except that section of it to the north over what had been the priory guest hall. This was left uncovered to be used as an open kitchen; it was re-roofed in the early 20th century.

Inside, substantial cross walls were added, with massive fireplaces and chimneys, creating three large rooms on the ground floor. The central of these was a hall, onto which the new front entrance opened. Here meals would have been taken and guests received. To the north was the kitchen, with a large inglenook fireplace, and to the south a parlour with a fine 17th-century fire surround. To the east (rear) a stair wing was added to access the first floor and attics. The oak stair balusters survive, as do, behind them, remains of the 17th-century red ochre decoration preserved by Bell here and elsewhere in the house.

On the first floor, above the parlour, was the main bedchamber. A corridor led to the other bedchambers, which were divided by timber-framed partitions. One of these survives, complete with its red ochre decoration.

Top: The stairs added to the house in the 17th century to give access to the upper floors. The oak balusters and the red ochre decoration remaining behind them are both preserved from that time

Above: The great inglenook fireplace in the 17th-century kitchen (now the English Heritage shop)

Left: The medieval guest house, later a residence, seen from the area of the Outer Court to the west

'You may hang your walls with tapestry instead of whitewash or paper; or you may cover them with mosaic, or have them frescoed by a great painter: all this is not luxury, if it be done for beauty's sake, and not for show: it does not break our golden rule: Have nothing in your houses which you do not know to be useful or believe to be beautiful' William Morris (above), speaking at the Birmingham Society of Arts and School of Design, 19 February 1880

Below: The entrance hall. The timber panelling and brass grate were installed between 1900 and 1901

A Tenanted Farmhouse

By the mid 18th century the estate was owned by the Mauleverer family of nearby Arncliffe Hall, who probably leased it out. Certainly by the end of the century the owner, Sarah Mauleverer, was leasing much of the estate to tenants. The main leaseholder was Christopher Bellwood, who lived with his family in the house from the 1770s. During his occupation the interior was altered to reflect contemporary tastes.

By the mid 19th century the house had been split into at least two residences and was described as a tenement in trade directories of the time. An extra staircase was built (later removed by Bell) in the kitchen (now the dining room) to allow separate access to the first floor. Cast-iron cooking ranges were put into the kitchen and entrance hall fireplaces, walls were papered and openings blocked.

The last of the Mauleverer family (see page 37) sold the estate to Sir Lowthian Bell in 1898. As a record Bell took a series of photographs, which show the dilapidated state of the interiors after many years as a tenanted farmhouse.

The Arts and Crafts House

Bell engaged the architect Ambrose Macdonald Poynter (1867–1923) to remodel the house in the Arts and Crafts style. As Poynter noted, the house 'was in a bad state of decay, and hardly more than a farmhouse, inhabited by a caretaker, whose cows grazed in the inner courtyard of the priory'.

Between 1900 and 1901 Poynter extended the house and exposed original medieval features, such as the hatches and doorways of the priory guest house. He also preserved and restored much of the 17th-century interiors. In the entrance hall he panelled the walls with reused, possibly 17th-century, timber panels. He replaced the 19th-century cast-iron range of

The Arts and Crafts Movement

The Arts and Crafts movement began in England in the mid 19th century in reaction to the rise of mass production. Its founder was the socialist artist and designer William Morris, who championed the hand of the craftsman in design. He drew for inspiration on medieval England and created everything from furniture to wallpaper, carpets, textiles, tapestries and bookbinding.

The Movement's focus was on simplicity of design, with ornamentation only if beautiful and suitable to the purpose, as opposed to the seemingly random ornamentation typical

Above: An Arts and Crafts chair in the drawing room. The wallpaper is a reproduction of the original by Morris & Co, called 'Double Bough'

of industrial objects. Furniture was simply crafted, but fabrics and wallpapers were exuberant and decorative.

Although socialist in its leanings, the Arts and Crafts movement was in many ways an upper-class trend, as few but the rich (such as Sir Lowthian Bell) could afford bespoke decorative objects. The socialism of Morris and his contemporaries was expressed instead in their desire for beauty in everyday objects. It was the 'Democracy of Art, the ennobling of daily and common work' that Morris hoped for.

the hall fireplace with a fashionable brass grate and lined the hearth with delft-type tiles. The kitchen Poynter converted into a dining room (now the shop), removed its 19th-century cast-iron range and reopened the 17th-century inglenook fireplace. He built new kitchen and service quarters beyond this new dining room, where there had been an open yard.

In the drawing room the north window was reopened, the stone-flagged floor replaced with timber, and a new large fireplace built into the original 17th-century surround. Today this room has been dressed as it may have appeared at the start of the 20th century, with wallpaper of the Morris & Co design 'Double Bough' reproduced from a surviving fragment of the original discovered behind the bookcase.

The room to the rear was known as the library, and was added on to the house in 1901. Here Poynter built a large stone fireplace with a raised shield bearing the arms of Bell and his wife, Margaret. Bell's coat-of-arms consists of three bells and three hawk lures. His wife's bears flames and silver droplets, a reference to the Pattinson process, a method of extracting silver from lead ore devised by Margaret's father, Hugh Lee Pattinson, for whom the arms were first created.

The first-floor bedrooms were refashioned, the bathroom extension added and the roof repaired and the attics divided to create further accommodation. In the 1920s these rooms were used as a nursery. One of the timber walls records the heights of three of the grandchildren of Sir Hugh Bell (see page 39): Hugh, John and Nora.

Below: The shield on the library fire surround bearing the coats-of-arms of Sir Lowthian Bell and his wife, Margaret

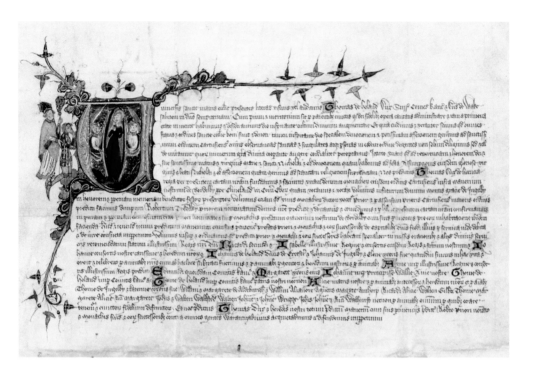

History of the Priory

FOUNDATION OF MOUNT GRACE PRIORY

Mount Grace Priory was founded by Thomas de Holand (c.1374–1400), 6th Earl of Kent and 1st Duke of Surrey and nephew of Richard II (r.1377–99), in 1398, following a licence granted by the king on 18 February of that year. The site of the priory, to be known as the house of Mount Grace of Ingleby, was to be de Holand's manor of Bordelbi, held of the king. The manor was tenanted by John de Ingleby, whose family had been resident in East Harlsey, of which Bordelbi was a part, since 1352. John de Ingleby and his wife, Eleanor, were associated with the foundation from the start.

The surviving foundation charter details de Holand's initial endowment, which comprised the 'alien' priories of Ware, Hinckley, Wareham and Carisbrooke, priories that had been seized from French houses during the Hundred Years War (1337–1453). The endowment was provided by Richard II in consideration of a payment of £1,000 from de Holand.

Grants of alien priories provided a substantial income at the time a new community was developing its site, but they were normally only to be held for the duration of hostilities with the relevant nation and were hardly a good foundation for a new community to build on. Yet the future of Mount Grace must have seemed assured, for the founder was one of the most powerful nobles in the kingdom, both on account of his great wealth and his close relationship with his uncle Richard II.

Above: Thomas de Holand's foundation charter of the priory, 1398, 'which he wishes to be called the house of Mount Grace of Ingleby'

Below: Seal of the foundation charter, bearing the arms of Thomas de Holand (c.1374–1400), 6th Earl of Kent and Duke of Surrey

Facing page: Illustration of Christ from a northern English Carthusian miscellany of poems, chronicles and treatises; produced at Mount Grace between 1460 and 1500

The Order of the Carthusians

The Carthusian order began in 1084 when St Bruno Hartenfaust, a canon and later chancellor of Reims in northern France, rejected what he deemed a corrupt Church.

THE BEGINNINGS

With a like-minded group of friends, Bruno sought the advice of St Robert of Molesme, the future founder of the Cistercian order, on the best way of withdrawing from the world to serve God.

Bruno soon left Robert, however, and with six of his companions decided to follow the example of St Anthony and his early community in Egypt. With the help of Bishop Hugh of Grenoble they settled at the Grande Chartreuse in the mountains of Haute Savoie. Here they lived as hermits in such austerity (early accounts tell of stark buildings, hair shirts and solitude) that by the early 12th century the monks of this new community were known as Christ's Poor Men.

Bruno had not intended to found a new monastic order. Numbers increased, however, and by 1117 it was necessary to adopt statutes to codify religious and social practice for the Grande Chartreuse and the eight other houses following the same eremitic tradition. The statutes were written by the fifth prior, Guigues du Pin, before 1133 at the request of his monks. They made the prior of the Grande Chartreuse the central authority of a new order, with an annual General Chapter to ensure the statutes were being properly interpreted and to amend them as necessary. The harsh and contemplative life of the monks has remained little changed to the present day.

ARRIVAL IN ENGLAND

As part of his penance for the death of Archbishop Thomas Becket, Henry II (r.1154–89) brought to England Carthusians from the Grande Chartreuse, settling them at Witham in Somerset. Here their third prior, St Hugh of Avalon (later

Bishop of Lincoln), firmly established the order.

A second house was founded from Witham by Henry II's bastard son William Longespee at Hatherop in Gloucestershire, but moved by William's widow to her park at Hinton near Bath in 1222.

The austere life of the Carthusians did not particularly appeal to the English, and for more than 150 years Witham and Hinton remained the only two Carthusian houses in England. In 1346 one of Edward III's captains in his French wars, Sir Nicholas de Cantilupe, founded before he went to war a third house, at Beauvale in his park at Greasley in Nottinghamshire.

It was the trauma of the Black Death of 1348 to 1349 and subsequent plague in 1362

that drew a demoralized population to the austere Carthusians. Sir Walter Maney, another of Edward III's captains, began this spiritual renaissance with his foundation of the London Charterhouse on a plague cemetery in 1371. Others followed suit, and in 1377 Hull was founded, Coventry in 1381, Axholme in 1397 to 1398, Mount Grace in 1398, and finally the royal charterhouse of Sheen in 1415.

In every case the founder came from the highest levels of society. The monks, too, came from the literate upper levels of society, some transferring from other orders, some starting as the chaplains of important landowners.

Above: St Bruno seeks the help of Bishop Hugh of Grenoble and founds the Grande Chartreuse, as depicted in a manuscript produced at Mount Grace between 1460 and 1500

Left: The Grande Chartreuse today, in the Haute Savoie mountains, France
Right: Effigy of William Longespee, bastard son of Henry II, on his tomb in Salisbury Cathedral. Longespee founded the second charterhouse in England, in Gloucestershire

Above: Two uncles of Thomas de Holand: John de Holand, 1st Duke of Exeter, and John Montagu, 3rd Earl of Salisbury (right), sent to confer with nobles on behalf of Richard II shortly before his deposition. Thomas de Holand and his uncle Salisbury were both beheaded by a mob at Cirencester in January 1400

Below: Richard II (r.1377–99), as depicted on a French manuscript presented to him in 1395

THE PRIORY IN THE 15TH CENTURY
The Founder Beheaded
Security was short-lived. Richard II was deposed in 1399 by Henry of Bolingbroke, son of John of Gaunt and grandson of Edward III, and the new king, Henry IV (r.1399–1413), deprived de Holand of his duchy and most of his influence. Following an abortive coup against Henry, de Holand was seized by the men of Cirencester following a skirmish there and beheaded on 9 or 10 January 1400, aged only about 26. Despite de Holand's treason, patronage of the priory passed to his surviving brother Edmund (1383–1408) and not to the Crown.

With the loss of their patron the monks at Mount Grace faced an uncertain future. They lost the grant of Ware, worth £251 a year. But Henry IV's intentions were apparently honourable: he made up at least part of the loss with an annual grant of £100 from the exchequer and a tun of Gascony wine, to be collected at Hull, until other lands could be granted.

The Monks Petition the King
The monks remained sufficiently uncertain of their claim to the priory site, however, that in 1412 they petitioned Henry IV to confirm their title. They stated that there were only nine monks and that they were unable to continue with their building work. The result of that petition is not known, but by 1438 Sir William de Ingleby acquired the patronage of the priory, apparently further alarming the monks over their position. The Inglebys had long been patrons of the nearby Augustinian priory of Gisborough and it had probably been at the insistence of Thomas de Holand, rather than the wish of William's ancestors John and Eleanor de Ingleby, that part of

the Ingleby lands was granted to the monks to found Mount Grace Priory in 1398. So in 1439, the monks again petitioned the king, now Henry VI (r.1422–61 and 1470–71), claiming that building had ceased with the death of their 'founder' (Thomas Beaufort; see below), who died on New Year's Eve 1426. This petition brought a royal confirmation in November 1440. But still the monks' position remained precarious.

A New Patron, Thomas Beaufort

The saviour of Mount Grace was Thomas Beaufort, Earl of Dorset and later Duke of Exeter, uncle of Henry V (r.1413–22). The king was establishing his own charterhouse at Sheen in 1415 and, looking for land with which to endow it, he considered taking Mount Grace's remaining alien priories. Beaufort, however, persuaded him to leave the estates of Hinckley Priory with Mount Grace in what was essentially a refoundation: his intention was to add a further five monks to the community, begin the construction of permanent cells, and to develop the church as his burial place.

In 1417 the General Chapter of the order granted Beaufort the right of burial in the priory church, and the church was extended and remodelled to make it a suitable burial place (see page 5). In 1421 he persuaded his nephew the king to make good the loss of the Ware estates (which Henry had given to Sheen), with the grant of four further alien priories: Hough, Minting and Long Bennington in Lincolnshire, and Field Dalling in Norfolk. Mount Grace must have subsequently approached the General Chapter about the poor state of their finances, because some time before 1437 Sheen agreed to pay the priory an annual £100 out of the profits of Ware until Mount Grace's new estates yielded a like income.

Above: The Beaufort arms, as borne by Thomas Beaufort (c.1377–1426), depicted in a French manuscript of the 15th century. The Beaufort motto appears on each of the scrolls: 'Me sovent sovant' (I remember often)
Below left: A coffin stands draped in black while monks in their stalls sing the office of the dead, as they would have done at Mount Grace; detail from a manuscript from Ghent, c.1516
Below: Remains of the church choir at Mount Grace; at the centre is the outline of a tomb, probably that of Thomas Beaufort, buried here in 1426

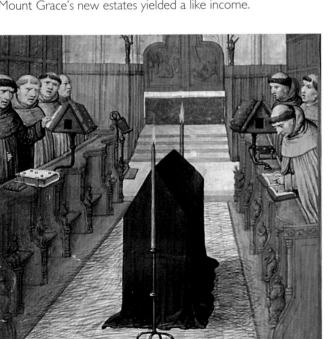

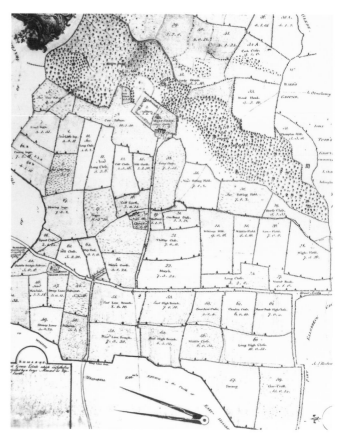

Above: A frieze from the infirmary hall of Rievaulx Abbey, probably from the late 15th century, showing a man on his way to a mill. Mount Grace had its own home farm, but rented another from Rievaulx

Right: Plan of the estate of Mount Grace drawn in 1768. It shows that the extent of the immediate lands acquired by the priory had changed little since the Suppression

Below: Edward IV (r.1461–70 and 1471–83), who granted estates to Mount Grace in 1462 and again in 1471, 15th-century portrait of the English school

THE EXPANSION OF THE PRIORY

Although the first half of the 15th century was an uncertain time for Mount Grace, the second half saw consolidation and growth. In 1449 Henry VI licensed Prior Robert Leek to acquire lands to the value of £40, indicating that the house was in a position to buy land for the first time. In 1456 Sir James and Dame Elizabeth Strangways of East Harlsey gave the church of Beighton near Sheffield to the priory. It was the first recorded endowment made by a local family to the priory and was to support it until its suppression. In 1462 and 1471, Edward IV granted further estates in Richmond and Warwickshire. Those in Richmond were to support a chantry for the king and his family. It was the last major grant to the priory.

These distant estates – leased out because the priory did not have staff to run them – provided the house with cash rents. Closer to home the priory had smaller holdings, most of which lay within a radius of 20 miles, and again provided the priory with cash rents. Only two of the 33 local estates generated an income above £10 per year, and ten were worth less than £1. The priory also had its adjacent home grange and rented another at East Harlsey from Rievaulx Abbey. The last prior, John Wilson was still trying to acquire new estates in the 1520s at a time of worsening inflation. With an annual income of £313 in 1535, however (almost the same as Rievaulx Abbey), the priory was not a poor house.

Left: The well house just outside the north-east corner of the Great Cloister. The conduit from it fed the water tower at the centre of the garth
Below: Drinking water was fed to each cell from the central water tower via lead pipes, as here, in the private cloister of the reconstructed cell
Bottom: Drawing of the cloister and well house of the monastery of La Verna in Italy, c.1607

Water for the Priory

Good drains and clean drinking water were central to Carthusian life, who, unlike other orders, drank water as well as beer. Various springs on the site provided water, some providing water to flush the drains, while three springs on the hillside were tapped to provide drinking water. Well houses were built over these three in the early 15th century.

The nearest of the well houses can be seen just outside the north-east corner of the Great Cloister. It fed an octagonal water tower, stone below and timber-framed above, at the centre of the Great Cloister. From here drinking water was distributed to each monk's cell by lead pipes, and to a laver in the south cloister alley for the monks to wash on entering and leaving their refectory.

Each cell had a latrine set over a channel flushed by running water. The latrines of Cells 1 to 5 were serviced by stone drains built within the area of the Great Cloister when it was first levelled, and flushed by springs in the cloister terrace itself. Cells 6 to 15 had latrines built over an open drain outside the precinct wall enclosing the Great Cloister. These were flushed by a spring on the hillside above the priory.

Two of the well houses are in the care of English Heritage: that which supplied the water tower in the Great Cloister, which is reached from the garden of Cell 4, and the one beyond it along the same path, which supplied the Lesser Cloister. The third, near the south-east corner of the priory, supplied the Inner Court and later the house. It is not managed by English Heritage.

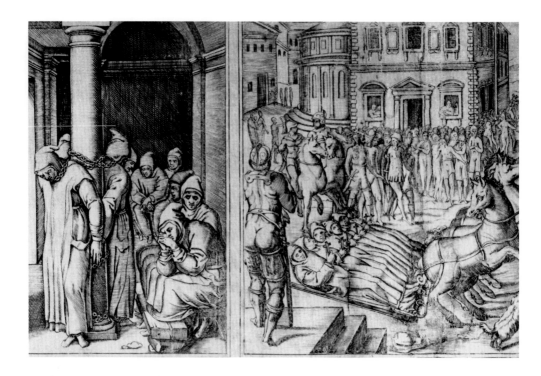

Top: The arrest and dragging away to execution of English Carthusian monks in 1535, from a print of 1564 depicting the history of the Carthusian order

Above: John Houghton, prior of the London Charterhouse, executed in 1535 for refusing to recognize Henry VIII as head of the Church; by Francisco de Zurbarán (1598–1664)

THE SUPPRESSION OF THE MONASTERIES
The Carthusians Resist

The destruction of the Carthusian congregation in England began before the Suppression of the Monasteries. It can be traced to the order's refusal to accept the Act of Succession of 1534, by which Henry VIII (r.1509–47) legitimized his second marriage despite the Pope's refusal to annul his first. By this Act all the king's subjects were required to swear an oath of acceptance, and Henry had hoped for the support of the Carthusians, whose opinion – with their great learning and writing in English as they did – carried weight. In fact, John Houghton, the prior of London Charterhouse, said it was not their concern: a matter of State not Church.

The Act of Succession was followed that same year by two more acts, the Act of Supremacy, which made the king 'the only supreme head in earth of the Church of England', and the Treason Act, which made denying any of the king's titles treason.

Prior Houghton, together with Robert Lawrence of Beauvale Charterhouse and Augustine Webster of Axholme Charterhouse asked to be exempted from taking an oath that the Act of Supremacy did not actually require, but thereby invoked the Treason Act and were subsequently tried and executed in May 1535. John Wilson, the prior of Mount Grace did accept the king's supremacy of the Church after taking the advice of the Archbishop of York and the Bishop of Durham, though two of his monks refused and fled to Scotland, only to be returned to Mount Grace and imprisoned. Mount Grace was to survive for another four years.

Pilgrimage of Grace

The suppression of the lesser monasteries, together with land reforms and rumours that the Government would turn next to the parish churches, led to open revolt in October 1536. It began in Lincolnshire, was quickly put down, but broke out more seriously in Yorkshire, with a strong input from the gentry.

The rebels marched under a banner of the Five Wounds of Christ, supported more or less willingly by the heads of a number of monasteries. They maintained that their target was the king's advisors, not the king himself, and required that the monasteries be restored.

The Duke of Norfolk was sent to deal with the rebels, finally meeting them at Doncaster, where, without a large enough army to stop them, he sought a truce. Their leader Robert Aske took their demands to the king in person. The outcome was a compromise, the rebels were pardoned and agreed to stand down. But the rebellion broke out again, the pardons were withdrawn and the Government took its revenge.

First the Lincolnshire rebels were dealt with: the abbots of Barlings, Bardney and Kirkstead abbeys were executed with a number of their monks, and their rich houses seized. In Yorkshire the prior of Bridlington and the abbot of Jervaulx together with the ex-prior of Gisborough and ex-abbot of Fountains were taken, and later tried, convicted of treason and executed. Bridlington and Jervaulx were seized; rich houses, they showed how much money would come to the Crown from the suppression of the greater houses and sealed their fate.

Above: An embroidered banner of the Five Wounds of Christ carried by one Thomas Constable on the Pilgrimage of Grace in 1536

Mount Grace Surrenders

The general suppression of the English monasteries began in 1536 when many houses with an annual income of less than £200 were closed, their inmates released or sent to greater monasteries, and their lands handed over to the king. None of the Carthusian houses were closed and in any case by this time Mount Grace had an income of £323. The closing of the smaller monasteries started two rebellions. The first was in Lincolnshire in October 1536, and was immediately followed by a second, the Pilgrimage of Grace, in Yorkshire. In both counties, major monasteries were caught up in the revolts, their presidents (abbots and priors) executed, and their estates seized over the course of 1537.

Below: A 16th-century 'memento mori' (reminder of death) made of bone. The other side has a woman's face. A similar bone head, depicting Christ, was found at Mount Grace

Above: Detail of a map of Bruges in 1562, by Marcus Gheeraerts the Elder, showing the charterhouse of Genadedal on the left just outside the city walls. It was here the exiled monks of the refounded house of Sheen (which included monks from several English houses, including Mount Grace) first sought refuge in 1558. The community eventually settled in Nieuwpoort, West Flanders

Below: Pottery bowl found at Mount Grace. In the garden of Cell 8 a pile of broken pottery was excavated, showing where a monk had thrown all his vessels against the wall before leaving at the Suppression

Mount Grace stayed out of this, but great houses such as Jervaulx and Bridlington were suppressed. Inevitably this led (the Crown realizing how much money was to be made) to a second round of suppressions, usually by persuasion, and the expelled monks were given reasonable pensions. The turn of Mount Grace came in December 1539. For signing the deed of surrender Prior John Wilson was given a pension of £60 a year and The Mount, a hermitage and chapel in Osmotherley, while 16 monks got annual pensions of between £16 13s. 4d. and £17, three novices £3 6s. 8d. and four lay brothers £2. Until the Suppression Mount Grace Priory had a full complement of monks in residence.

Later Prior John Wilson, Sir Leonard Hall (a monk), and two lay brothers, who had doubtless been living quietly at The Mount, joined Sheen Charterhouse which was refounded in 1555 under Queen Mary (r.1553–8). In 1558, Elizabeth I (r.1558–1603) suppressed Sheen for a second time and the community finally settled at Nieuwpoort in West Flanders.

THE PRIORY FALLS INTO RUIN

Once closed Mount Grace's movable possessions were sold and its partial demolition began. The monks seem to have taken the contents of their cells with them, as the monks did at the London Charterhouse. In the garden of Cell 8 an excavated pile of broken pottery showed where the departing monk had thrown all his table vessels one by one against the cell wall – in anger, presumably. Some of the pottery was a valuable southern European type, and, unable to carry it with him, he evidently preferred not to leave it to his evictors. Buildings were unroofed and some demolished, probably to sell off the building materials, but the priory guest house was left to form the nucleus of a house.

The site and its local estates were leased in the name of the king by the Court of Augmentations, which managed the

Suppression of the Monasteries, first to John Cheney, a dealer in monastic lands, and then to Sir James Strangways who acquired the freehold in 1541. Strangways died that year, and Mount Grace passed to his cousin Robert Ross who sold it to Ralph Rokeby in 1545. At this time the priory may have been tenanted, its buildings probably put to agricultural use.

Rokeby's son William gave 'the remains of the dissolved abby of Mountgrace' as a marriage settlement to his granddaughter Grace upon her marriage to Conyers, Lord Darcy (c.1598–1689) in October 1616. It is probably at this time and by Lord Darcy, described in records as 'of Mount Grace', that the building was substantially altered to form a residence for Darcy and his wife.

THE LASCELLES FAMILY

In 1653 Darcy succeeded his father as the 8th Lord Darcy of Knayth, and 5th Lord Conyers, and sold Mount Grace to Captain Thomas Lascelles (1624–c.1658), who had fought in the Civil War (1642–51) on the Parliamentarian side. Darcy moved with his wife to the much grander Hornby Castle near Richmond. It was once thought, given the initials TL and date 1654 above the entrance to Mount Grace, that it was Lascelles who first converted the guest house into a residence. But the indenture for the sale records that Darcy sold a 'capital messuage' (main dwelling house) with other 'houses, buildings, barns, stables, dovecote, out houses, gardens, tofts', suggesting Darcy had already fully developed and converted the house.

The estate passed to Lascelles' wife at his death and then in 1672, following a legal dispute, to his grandson, also Thomas, who was the last of the Lascelles to live at Mount Grace. Thomas's successor, William Lascelles, lived at Crossgates in Durham. In his will dated 1722 William bequeathed the estate to his wife, Alice Woodmass, and its management to his cousin Timothy Mauleverer (c.1680–1753) of Ingleby Arncliffe Hall. A sketch by Samuel Buck of that year shows the priory and house at the time, although with many inaccuracies, such as

Above: Conyers, Lord Darcy (later 1st Earl of Holdernesse), in about 1630 by Johannes Priwitzer. It was probably Darcy, described as 'of Mount Grace' and his wife, Grace Rokeby, who altered the medieval guest house to form a residence after their marriage in 1616

Below: An engraving from a sketch by Samuel Buck of the west view of Mount Grace Priory in 1722, the year William Lascelles bequeathed the estate to his wife and his cousin Timothy Mauleverer. The engraving is highly fanciful – the church incorrectly positioned, and the house having four, rather than three, dormers

four, rather than the original three (now two), dormers. The estate passed to William's son the Reverend Robert Lascelles (c.1721–1801), known as 'Panty' after Rabelais' comic character Pantegruel. He was a member of the group the Demoniacs, together with Laurence Sterne and John Hall Stevenson. It was Robert who sold Mount Grace in 1744 to Timothy Mauleverer.

Mauleverer probably leased the estate to tenants rather than living there. His son Thomas inherited the estate. In 1768 he had an estate plan drawn up that notes that 'Mount Grace Estate which is tythe free is surrounded by a large upcast of earth'. This raised boundary follows the current parish borders

Top: The ruins of Mount Grace Priory in 1842, by William Richardson, much as it appeared some 50 years later, when it was described as 'in a bad state of decay, and hardly more than a farmhouse, inhabited by a caretaker, whose cows grazed in the inner courtyard of the priory'

Above: The Reverend Robert 'Panty' Lascelles out fishing. Robert sold the priory to his father's cousin Timothy Mauleverer in 1744

Right: The west front of the Mount Grace house, as it appeared at about the time it was bought by Sir Lowthian Bell in 1898

and probably indicates the extent of the monastic lands or even the earlier Bordelbi manor.

Mount Grace descended through the Mauleverer family to William Brown, a historian with a particular interest in Yorkshire monasteries. Brown helped to record the history of the priory from original documents and invited the leading monastic archaeologist Sir William St John Hope to excavate the site in 1896. In 1898 Brown sold the estate to the successful industrialist Sir Isaac Lowthian Bell (1816–1904).

A COUNTRY HOUSE

Sir Lowthian Bell was one of the most influential figures to own Mount Grace. His main residence, from 1876, was at nearby Rounton Grange, a large country house designed for Bell by his friend the architect Philip Webb with furniture by the designer William Morris. Bell had made a large fortune in the chemical, iron and steel industries in the north-east of England and become a patron of the arts, particularly of the Pre-Raphaelite Brotherhood and the Arts and Crafts movement.

In 1886 the committee of the Society for the Protection of Ancient Buildings (SPAB) wrote to Bell of their concern over the eventual fate of the priory ruins. It asked Bell to 'form an association for the purposes of buying this [Mount Grace Priory] and to place it in the trust of some public body'. Bell assured SPAB of his 'hearty co-operation', and spoke to the owner, William Brown, of Arncliffe Hall, who agreed that the ruins should be preserved; but SPAB's letter had ignited Bell's interest and by 1898 he had bought not only the priory ruins, but the whole Arncliffe estate. He and his architect Ambrose

The Redcar Carpet

The carpet in the drawing room (see above; on loan from the Bell family) was commissioned by Hugh Bell (see page 39) in 1881 from William Morris. It originally adorned Hugh's drawing room at Red Barns, his house in Redcar designed by Philip Webb. The carpet's design and manufacture are typical of Morris: intertwining flowers and vegetation, bold colours, traditional weaving techniques and natural dyes. In the corner near the door is the distinctive trademark (see below) of Morris's workshop in the coach house of his Hammersmith home.

The Redcar carpet was the largest woven in this workshop, which was not well suited for such output. Soon after it was made Morris moved his operation from Hammersmith to Merton Abbey.

Sir Lowthian Bell (above),
writing to the Society for
the Protection of Ancient
Buildings about the ruins of
Mount Grace in 1886

Macdonald Poynter (1869–1923) then began sympathetic work
on the house, using traditional materials and techniques in the
spirit of the Arts and Crafts Movement. The work was
completed in 1901.

For the next 30 years Mount Grace became a sort of
weekend retreat for the Bell family, their friends and associates
for entertaining and shooting parties. On Sir Lowthian's death
in 1904 his son (Thomas) Hugh Bell (1844–1931) inherited.
Hugh was married to the author and playwright Florence Bell,
and a guest book from the period includes the names of many
eminent visitors, such as Charles Peers, the Chief Inspector of
Ancient Monuments, and the author John Buchan and his
fiancée Susan Grosvenor, who visited in September 1906.

In 1927 the Mount Grace Pageant, a celebration of the
history of the priory, was held in the grounds. It was written by
Florence and her close friend the actress Elizabeth Robins
delivered the prologue. The pageant was performed over
three days at a cost of £1,800, with a cast of 1,279 characters in
medieval costume, and proved immensely popular: over 400

*Top: The workmen who refurbished
and extended Mount Grace for
Sir Lowthian Bell, posing in front of
the house in about 1900*
*Right: Photograph of the kitchen of
the tenement before it was converted
into Sir Lowthian Bell's dining room. It
is now the English Heritage shop*

Gertrude Bell

Gertrude Bell (1868–1926), granddaughter of Sir Lowthian Bell and daughter of his son Hugh, was a remarkable woman: scholar, archaeologist, botanist, explorer, diplomatist, and in all of which, recalled her stepmother 'she was recognised by experts as an expert'. In 1871 Gertrude's mother died giving birth to Gertrude's brother Maurice. Gertrude developed a close relationship with her father which lasted the rest of her life.

At 17 Gertrude went to Oxford: a 'vivid, rather untidy, auburn-haired girl' noted a contemporary, who 'took our hearts by storm with her brilliant talk and her youthful confidence'. She went on to conduct archaeological expeditions, such as that in the Arabian Peninsula, where she recorded the Roman and Byzantine forts along the Euphrates. Her extensive knowledge of the Middle East, its people and culture proved invaluable; she became a diplomatic advisor and helped to shape the post-First World War settlement of the region and notably the creation of the Kingdom of Iraq.

Gertrude spent her childhood at her family home, Red Barns, in Redcar, and at her grandfather's house at Rounton Grange. She knew Mount Grace well and mentions it often in her letters, as in 1903, when she wrote from Japan to Sir Hugh: 'Father! you are the Lord of 110 trees! Japanese cherries and plums, not dwarfed. I think we shall have to induce our respected father and grandfather to let us make a plantation at R'ton or Mt Grace – wouldn't it be nice to have a Japanese cherry grove! They have cost you about £2.10s. with carriage.' Some may have been planted in the priory orchard.

Above: Photograph of Gertrude Bell at the age of 53
Below left: Gertrude with her father, Sir Hugh Bell, in 1876 by Sir Edward John Poynter
Below: Gertrude (right), with her half-sisters Molly (foreground) and Elsa, and their father Sir Hugh Bell at Mount Grace Priory in 1900

people attended one of the dress rehearsals alone and it was filmed and a short excerpt shown in cinemas in Northallerton.

The fortunes of the Bell family declined between the wars. By the 1930s their main house at Rounton Grange had become a drain on their resources and was closed. Finally, after failed attempts to sell it, it was demolished in 1953. Sir Hugh Bell's son, Maurice (1871–1944) took up permanent residence at Mount Grace in 1932 and lived there until his death.

*Above: Excavations at Mount Grace
Priory in 1957*
*Below: The house from the south-west
in threatening weather*

MOUNT GRACE TODAY

After Sir Maurice Bell's death in 1944 the priory was given to the treasury in lieu of death duties. In the early 1950s there was speculation that the priory was to be bought back by the Carthusian order and restored to its original use, but instead it was given to the National Trust. The house itself continued to be occupied by a tenant until the 1970s. In 1955 the Trust placed the site into the Guardianship of the State and in 1957 the Ministry of Works began excavations. The two well houses to the north-east of the priory (see page 31) were discovered in 1958. They were fully excavated and restored in 1965; the date is carved on a replacement stone on each well house.

The last tenant at Mount Grace was Miss Kathleen Cooper Abbs, who drowned in 1974 at the age of 73 attempting to swim around Saltburn pier to raise money for local churches. The house empty, the Ministry now turned its attention there. It had suffered neglect and changes since its restoration in 1901: the Morris wallpapers had been painted over in several rooms and there was dry and wet rot, which required the closure, stripping, and repair of most of the building. Restoration began in 1987 and upon completion in 2010 the house was opened again to the public.